FROM SEA to SHINING SEA

KENTUCKY

SUZANNE M. WILLIAMS

Consultants

MELISSA N. MATUSEVICH, PH.D.
Curriculum and Instruction Specialist
Blacksburg, Virginia

ANNE HALL
Youth Services Librarian
Clark County Public Library
Winchester, Kentucky

CHILDREN'S PRESS®
AN IMPRINT OF SCHOLASTIC INC.

New York • Toronto • London • Auckland • Sydney • Mexico City
New Delhi • Hong Kong • Danbury, Connecticut

Kentucky is located in the South. Other southern states include Alabama, Arkansas, Delaware, Florida, Georgia, Louisiana, Maryland, Mississippi, North Carolina, South Carolina, Tennessee, Virginia, and West Virginia.

Project Editor: Lewis K. Parker
Design Director: Marie O'Neill
Photo Researcher: Marybeth Kavanagh
Design: Robin West, Ox and Company
Page 6 map and recipe art: Susan Hunt Yule
All other maps: XNR Productions, Inc.

Library of Congress Cataloging-in-Publication Data

Williams, Suzanne, 1949–
    Kentucky / by Suzanne M. Williams.
      p. cm.—(From sea to shining sea)
    Includes bibliographical references and index.
    ISBN 13: 978-0-531-20805-2
    ISBN 10: 0-531-20805-2
    1. Kentucky—Juvenile literature. I. Title

F451.3 .W54 2008
976.9—dc22   2007©46537

TABLE of CONTENTS

CHAPTER ONE

INTRODUCING THE BLUEGRASS STATE

Thoroughbred horses are seen throughout Kentucky.

Kentucky is called the Bluegrass State. Is the grass blue? Yes, if it's long enough. Adult bluegrass will produce blue seeds, which can make a field of it look blue. Bluegrass is just the beginning. Things aren't always what you might expect in Kentucky. The commonwealth, as the state is officially called, has a cave large enough in which to hold a concert. Kentucky also has the world's tallest, fastest, longest stand-up roller coaster. You can even find a museum for baseball bats in this state.

Kentucky is a land of opposites. In Kentucky, you can see cars being made in a modern factory one day and the next day, listen to someone explain how to make shoes the old-fashioned way. Abraham Lincoln, the sixteenth president, was born in Kentucky, and so was Jefferson Davis, the president of the Confederate states.

Kentucky is also a state for people who love horses. Kentucky Thoroughbreds are famous around the world. Kentucky is home of the

American Saddlebred, a truly American breed. Every year, racing fans flock to the Kentucky Derby. Many families visit Kentucky Horse Park, the only horse theme park in the world.

Kentuckians love music and athletics. Bill Monroe, the father of bluegrass music, came from Kentucky. So did country singer Loretta Lynn and a few members of the Backstreet Boys. Kentucky is also the birthplace of many athletes, such as basketball player Wes Unsold, and heavyweight boxing champion Muhammad Ali.

What can you find in Kentucky?

❖ Trails where Daniel Boone led frontier people through the wilderness

❖ Civil War battlefields where Union and Confederate soldiers fought

❖ People exploring the underground wonders of Mammoth Cave

❖ The sound of banjos and fiddles from country musicians

❖ Stacks of gold bars at Fort Knox

❖ Southern mansions with tall pillars

❖ Canoe riders on rivers and lakes

❖ Fans watching the Kentucky Derby

How do you squeeze all that into the thirty-seventh largest state? What would Daniel Boone, Kentucky's frontier hero, think of the state today? He'd be surprised and so might you.

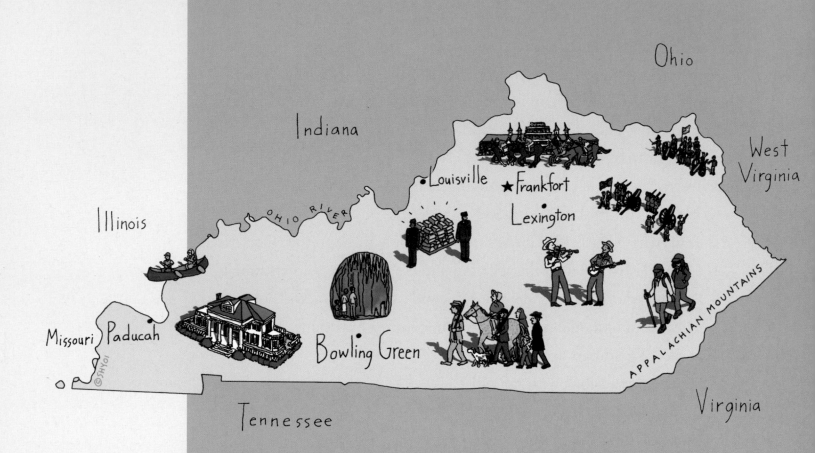

Ohio

Indiana

West
Virginia

Illinois

OHIO RIVER

•Louisville ★Frankfort
Lexington

Missouri Paducah

©SHY01

Bowling Green

APPALACHIAN MOUNTAINS

Tennessee

Virginia

CHAPTER TWO

THE LAND OF KENTUCKY

If you were to ask three people to send postcards from Kentucky, the first card might show mountains, rippling creeks, and thick forests. The second might picture horses grazing in gentle pastures. In the third photo, you could see barges floating through reflections of city lights on the Ohio River. All three postcards are different, but they are all true pictures of Kentucky.

If you look at Kentucky on a map, you might think that it looks like a cat ready to pounce. Its head and arched back are along the Ohio River, and its paws are by the Mississippi.

Kentucky borders seven states: Tennessee is to the south and Virginia to the southeast. West Virginia is to the northeast across the Big Sandy River. Missouri is to the west across the Mississippi River. Indiana, Illinois, and Ohio are north of Kentucky across the Ohio River.

Kentucky has (40,409 square miles (104,659) square kilometers) of land. Kentucky runs 458 miles (737 km) from east to west and 171

This view captures a glimpse of Kentucky's beauty.

miles (275 km) north to south. The state is so wide that it has two time zones. The eastern part of the state uses Eastern Time while the western part uses Central Time.

REGIONS

Kentuckians think of the state as having five geographic regions. Starting in the east is the Eastern Coal Field. It is named for the coal mined in the Cumberland Mountains, a part of the Appalachian Mountain chain. The Eastern Coal Field is a mountain area with forests, creeks, small towns, and farms. Kentucky's highest point, Black Mountain, is in the Eastern Coal Field. This mountain is 4,145 feet (1,264 meters) high.

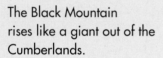

The Black Mountain rises like a giant out of the Cumberlands.

The Bluegrass Region is in the middle of the state just west of the Eastern Coal Field. This area is famous for strong, fast horses and fertile farms. Visitors to the area see farmhouses and pastures with white and black fences. As bluegrass grows in late May, it looks bluish. The cities of Louisville, Lexington, and Frankfort (the capital) are in the Bluegrass Region. Bluegrass isn't from Kentucky at all. It was probably brought from England to Kentucky sometime after 1785. Legends say that it was brought in a thimble, started from a bale of hay, or carried by hand into Clark County.

Rolling hills and horse farms are found in the Bluegrass Region.

The Pennyroyal area curves around the Bluegrass, to the south and west. It is named for a little blue flower that grows wild there. Many rivers in the Pennyroyal run underground, forming Kentucky's famous caves. Northwest of the Pennyroyal, along the 981-mile (1,579-km) Ohio River is the Western Coal Field. You guessed it. People mine coal there. The area is also a rich source of natural gas and oil.

The Jackson Purchase is in the western corner of the state. President Andrew Jackson bought this low-lying farming area from the Chickasaw nation of Native Americans in 1818. This area is swampy, with many

FIND OUT MORE

The seeds of bluegrass may have traveled from England to Kentucky. How do plants travel to new places? Are there any that have "hitch-hiked" to your area? What effect have these plants had?

13,124 ft. — 4,000 m
6,562 ft. — 2,000 m
4,921 ft. — 1,500 m
3,281 ft. — 1,000 m
1,640 ft. — 500 m
820 ft. — 250 m
0 — 0

N

INDIANA

OHIO

BLUEGRASS
REGION

Frankfort

Louisville

Big Sandy R.

WEST
VIRGINIA

ILLINOIS

WESTERN
COAL FIELD

Ohio R.

Salt R.

Kentucky R.

EASTERN
COAL FIELD

N. Fk. Kentucky R.

S. Fk.
Kentucky R.

VIRGINIA

Green R.

Lake
Barkley

PENNYROYAL
REGION

Lake
Cumberland

Cumberland R.

Black Mtn.
4,145 ft. /
1,264 m

MISSOURI

Kentucky
Lake

JACKSON
PURCHASE
REGION

Mississippi R.

CUMBERLAND MTS.

CUMBERLAND GAP

0   20   40 mi.

0   20   40 km

TENNESSEE

10

ponds. Kentucky's lowest point, 257 feet (78 m), is here in Fulton County near the Mississippi River. The Mississippi, which runs from Minnesota to New Orleans, divides Kentucky from Missouri. The way the river curves at New Madrid Bend means the west corner of Kentucky isn't connected to the rest of the state at all!

In 1811 and 1812, powerful earthquakes struck the New Madrid area. The earthquakes were so severe that they actually changed the course of the Mississippi River for a period of time. A man named James Fletcher was traveling on a riverboat around this time. He wrote, "The earth was . . . entirely inundated [filled] with water. . . . I heard that many parts of the Mississippi River had caved in; in some places, several acres at the same instant." This region still has earthquakes.

The Kentucky River winds through these forested hills.

WATER

Although Kentucky is far from any ocean, water connects it to the world. Kentucky has more miles of rivers and streams (89,431 miles or 143,925 km) than any state except Alaska. Rivers such as the Ohio, Mississippi, Green, Cumberland, and Kentucky have carried people and cargo for generations. These rivers carved canyons in the east,

FIND OUT MORE

Mammoth Cave was created by rivers. How might water help create caves? What is a stalagmite? What is a stalactite? How are these formed in caves?

wandered through fields in the west, and flowed underground in the south, where they created caves. Hundreds of people every year visit Cumberland Falls, along the Cumberland River, to see "moonbows." These nighttime rainbows happen only within a few days of a full moon. The longest cave system in the world, Mammoth Caves (more than 350 miles of known caves or 563 km), is also in Kentucky. At Natural Bridge in the Appalachian Mountains, a 65-foot (20-m) sandstone bridge formed by wind and water erosion arches high above the Red River in Powell County.

FORESTS AND EARTH

Forests cover about half of Kentucky. It has 12.7 million acres (51,395 sq km) of trees. These forests make Kentucky a very green state.

Forests have also done something else for Kentucky. Within the last two hundred years, Kentucky has produced more than 7.4 billion tons (6.71 billion metric tons) of coal. Coal was created millions of years ago when land in today's Kentucky was close to the equator. Tropical forests grew in the hot, steamy climate. Through millions of years, continents on earth moved and those forests died. Over a long period of time, rising seas and mud covered the trees. The buried plants gradually changed to coal. Today, Kentucky miners take billions of dollars worth of coal from mines. In

EXTRA! EXTRA!

In the Bluegrass Region, limestone is close to the surface. Grass that grows in limestone soil is rich in important minerals such as calcium. Kentucky's horses, cows, and other livestock grow up strong and healthy because they eat this grass.

1998, only two states produced more coal than Kentucky's 130.6 million tons (118.4 million metric tons).

More than half the rocks in Kentucky are made of limestone. This kind of rock made Kentucky famous. How? Water and limestone together created an underground system of caves and sinks. This type of land formation is referred to as "karst." Just over half of Kentucky sits above this kind of ground.

Coal is loaded onto train cars and transported to destinations throughout the country.

CLIMATE

Kentucky doesn't feel like the tropics anymore. Kentucky has a moderate climate. Summer weather is influenced by warm air coming from the Gulf of Mexico. Winter weather is caused mainly by powerful storms.

Kentucky's hottest day ever was in 1930, when the temperature hit 114° Fahrenheit (46° Celsius). The coldest recorded temperature was -37°F (-38°C), in 1994. Don't expect those temperatures every day. Louisville and Lexington average 87°F (31°C) in the summer and 22°F (-6° C) in the winter. These cities receive about 44.5 inches (113 centimeters) of rain every year and sometimes snow in the winter. In Kentucky, wear your shorts in the summer, your coat in the winter, and keep the umbrella handy.

FIND OUT MORE

In ancient times, the land that is now called Kentucky was actually located near the equator. How do scientists think land moves across thousands of miles? How fast does it travel? Can you feel it move?

CHAPTER THREE

KENTUCKY THROUGH HISTORY

The remains of mastodons are found at Big Bone Lick State Park.

The remains of mammoths and giant sloths poke out of the ground at Big Bone Lick State Park near Covington. Once, only prehistoric animals like these thumped through Kentucky forests and splashed in Kentucky rivers. No people lived here then.

More than eleven thousand years ago, people arrived. Their ancestors came from northeast Asia. These people hunted, picked nuts and berries, and used stone and bone tools. About three thousand years ago, Woodland People, called Adena and Hopewell, started raising gourds and squash. They buried their dead in large mounded graves. They made pottery and traded with other tribes.

By A.D. 900, groups called Mississippian and Fort Ancient lived along Kentucky rivers. Like earlier Adena/Hopewell people, the Mississippian and Fort Ancients grew squash and gourds. They also raised corn. Corn was easy to grow and to store. This dependable food allowed Fort Ancient and Mississippian groups to settle in one place. They often built their villages in the same areas where the Adena/Hopewell villages had once been.

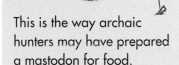

This is the way archaic hunters may have prepared a mastodon for food.

Mississippian and Fort Ancient people disappeared between 1500 and 1700. What happened to them? No one knows for sure. Today, their burial mounds still mark the land. By the time European explorers came into what is now Kentucky, no Native Americans lived there. Tribes such as the Delaware, the Shawnee, and the Cherokee used the area now called Kentucky as a hunting ground.

Jacques Marquette of France explored along the Mississippi River.

NATIVE AMERICANS AND NEWCOMERS

In the 1600s, Great Britian, France, and Spain all claimed parts of North America. They sent explorers and colonists to the "new" land. The British built colonies on the coast. French trappers worked near

EXTRA! EXTRA!

In 1682 René-Robert Cavelier explored the Louisiana Territory for France. The area now called Kentucky was claimed by France. In 1776 France built a trading post in Kentucky on the Ohio River.

North American rivers, claiming land along the Mississippi and Ohio Rivers for France. By the middle of the 1700s, British colonists on the coast wanted more farmland. However, the Appalachian Mountains were a barrier that made traveling west very difficult.

In 1749 a group of Virginians formed the Loyal Company. They hoped to sell land west of the Appalachians to settlers. They hired Dr. Thomas Walker to find a way through the mountains. In 1750 he found a pass through the mountains that he called the Cumberland Gap. He named it after the English duke of Cumberland. This pass was wide enough for a packed mule but not wide enough for a wagon. Over the next twenty years, the Cumberland Gap would become the main route for settlers traveling into Kentucky.

The Loyal Company's plans, however, were interrupted by war. In 1754, Great Britian and France fought the French and Indian War (1754– 1763). Both countries wanted control of North America. Each country wanted Native American groups to join their side.

At first, the Shawnee did not take sides. Another Native American tribe, the Iroquois, joined the British and "gave" them Ohio. The Shawnee and Delaware tribes were angry. They lived in Ohio too. The Iroquois had no right to give away land that didn't belong to them. In July 1755 the Shawnee sent messengers to Pennsylvania to protest the agreement. Many colonists in Pennsylvania were angry because a thousand British soldiers had just been killed in a battle with a different tribe. Some of the colonists seized the Shawnee messengers and hanged them.

Angered by how their messengers had been treated, the Shawnee attacked settlements in Pennsylvania, Virginia, and Maryland.

On July 8, 1755, a band of Shawnee attacked Mary Ingles's homestead in Virginia. They captured her, her two sons, and her sister-in-law and took them to Kentucky. Mary, who was pregnant, had her baby during the trip. Once in Kentucky, Mary was adopted as a chief's daughter. That fall, Mary escaped, but she had to leave her baby behind. After forty days, she found her way home. One of her sons died. The other son was reunited with his family in 1768.

In 1763 the British won the French and Indian War. With the French gone, many British colonists wanted to move west of the Appalachians. However, King George III of England issued the Proclamation of 1763, which stated that no one was allowed to move west of the mountains.

Despite the Proclamation, hunters began making trips into Kentucky to shoot deer for their valuable skins. These hunters stayed months at a time. Because of their long trips, they were called long hunters. Daniel Boone was a long hunter. His first trip to Kentucky lasted from 1769 to 1771.

In 1774, James Harrod and some friends from Pennsylvania built a fort and some cabins in Kentucky. They called the settlement

Harrodsburg. This town became Kentucky's first permanent white settlement. Others built cabins nearby. The Shawnee were not pleased that settlers were establishing homes in their hunting grounds. They attacked the settlers. In turn, settlers destroyed Shawnee camps.

On October 10, 1774, Virginia's governor, Lord Dunmore, led 1,300 men into battle against the Shawnee at Point Pleasant, Virginia. The Shawnee, led by Chief Cornstalk, were outnumbered. They retreated. In the Treaty of Camp Charlotte, the Shawnee agreed to stop hunting south of the Ohio River. In turn, settlers promised to live only south of the river.

After Dunmore's War, Kentucky was safer for settlers. They built forts or stations. Most stations were home to just a few families. One man had bigger plans. Judge Richard Henderson imagined a new colony in Kentucky. However, the British had issued the Proclamation of 1763, which outlawed settling in Kentucky and other lands west of the Appalachians. According to laws in Virginia and North Carolina, it was illegal to buy land from Native Americans.

In January 1775, Henderson organized the Transylvania Company. He hired Daniel Boone to bargain with the Cherokee leaders. In March, the Cherokees "sold" much of eastern Kentucky to the Transylvania Company.

Daniel Boone and Henderson founded Boonesborough in March 1775. Settlers built cabins in rows with walls between the cabins to protect them from attacks. Native Americans who had not sold the land attacked the settlers, but the first settlers held on.

AMERICAN REVOLUTION

The French and Indian War was expensive for Great Britain. To help pay for the extra cost, Great Britain forced the colonists to pay high taxes, charging them extra money on everything from newspapers to molasses. Each year there were new British taxes and stricter laws. Colonists said only their own governments should pass taxes and make laws. The colonies wanted to be free from Britain's rule. After years of arguing, riots, and shootings, the American Revolution (1775–1783) began.

During the war, British officers encouraged Native Americans to attack the settlers. The Shawnee sided with the British, attacking many colonists in Kentucky. Because of attacks, fewer than two hundred settlers stayed in Kentucky. They fought both British soldiers and Native Americans.

After the American Revolution, Virginia paid its soldiers with deeds to land in Kentucky. Daniel Boone supervised widening the Cumberland Gap trail so a wagon could pass. New settlers poured into the state. By 1800, Kentucky had more than 200,000 people.

This drawing shows Native Americans preparing to attack Logan's Fort.

In February 1778, the Shawnee captured Daniel Boone at Lower Blue Licks. Blackfish, the chief of the tribe, adopted Boone as a son and named him Big Turtle. Boone escaped and returned to Boonesborough. In September, Blackfish led four hundred Shawnee in an attack on Boonesborough. Boonesborough didn't surrender, and eight days later the Shawnee retreated.

Native Americans united and fought hard to stop the stream of newcomers. However, more and more settlers moved into Kentucky. The Shawnee and other tribes were eventually pushed to Ohio and, in later years, to Missouri, Kansas, and Oklahoma.

Great Britain and the United States fought again in the War of 1812 (1812–1814). During the war, Kentuckians fought British and Native Americans. Two out of every three Americans killed in that war were from Kentucky.

FROM FRONTIER TO FARMLAND

The Cumberland Gap was the main land pathway into Kentucky. However, the real highway was the Ohio River. Families packed their goods onto flatboats in Pittsburgh, Pennsylvania, where the Ohio River began. They floated down the river on boats loaded with chickens, dogs, and household goods.

Flatboats were used to move people and cargo up and down the river. They were pushed by poles.

Around 1789, a Baptist minister, Elijah Craig, probably developed the first bourbon whiskey in Kentucky. Bourbon is made from corn. Bourbon was easier to transport and worth more than the corn used to make it. Before long, making bourbon became an important business in Kentucky.

With few roads, the river was the easiest way to deliver crops to market, too. Going downstream was easy. but coming back was hard. Tobacco, which was easy to store and carry, and livestock, that could walk to market, became important products. Kentucky settlers made most of what they needed. Women made soap, candles, and cloth. Children were taught at home or in small community or church schools.

Kentuckians always made time for fun, too. Frontier weddings in particular, called for huge celebrations. Even the completion of a log cabin led to hours of feasting, music, and dance.

In colonial Kentucky, whole communities gathered together to celebrate a wedding.

STATEHOOD

In the late 1700s, Kentucky was a county of the new state of Virginia. Soon, Kentuckians grew tired of sending their tax money to Virginia. They argued that their money was being spent in Virginia and not in Kentucky. In 1792 the government agreed. Kentucky became its own state and joined the United States as the fifteenth state.

Soon after Kentucky became a state, steam-powered machines were invented that made life easier. A Kentuckian, John Fitch, patented the first steamboat model in 1791. Fitch didn't have enough money to build a working boat but Robert Fulton did in 1810. Steamboats now carried freight in and out of Kentucky's ports. Railroads carried goods and people over land. The work of many people, together with the power of new machines, turned Kentucky's meadows and trails into farms and cities.

WHO'S WHO IN KENTUCKY?

Catherine Spalding (1793–1858). In 1812 she helped start the Sisters of Charity of Nazareth in Bardstown. The order of Roman Catholic nuns opened schools for Catholic families who had moved to Kentucky. Their order is still active.

With the coming of steamboats, Louisville, Covington, Paducah, and other cities on the Ohio River became important ports.

African Americans, such as Molly Logan and her sons, were among Kentucky's first pioneers. They arrived, in 1776, with Benjamin Logan's family. They helped build Logan's Fort. They also helped defend it from Native American attacks. Molly and Benjamin's wife, Ann, even made bullets for the settlers to use in their rifles.

Because slavery was not illegal in Kentucky, many settlers brought African Americans along as slaves. By 1830 almost one of every four Kentuckians was an African-American slave. As in other southern states, slaves did the hardest work. Enslaved people worked at doing daily chores, clearing land, and building cabins. They could be punished for not pleasing their masters or for trying to escape. enslaved African Americans were treated as property and could be bought and sold.

Kentucky's population of enslaved people grew. Farmers often sold slaves they didn't need to work on their farms. Between 1830 and 1860, at least 77,000 captives were taken from their families and "sold down the river" to work on large plantations, or farms, on the lower Mississippi River.

Some enslaved African Americans tried to escape. In 1829, while slave traders were taking about sixty captives to Vanceburg to be sold down the river, they escaped their chains and turned on the slave traders. Law officers caught most of the slaves. In 1848,

WHAT'S IN A NAME?

The names of many places in Kentucky have interesting origins.

Name	Comes from or means
Cumberland	England's Duke of Cumberland
Henderson	Colonel Richard Henderson
Louisville	King Louis XVI of France
Lexington	Named in 1775 for the Battle of Lexington
Paducah	Chickasaw Chief Paduke

another revolt occurred. Edward Doyle gave weapons to fifty-five enslaved African Americans and led an escape near Maysville. Again, most of them were later captured.

The Ohio River divided Kentucky from the free states in the North, where slavery was illegal. African Americans who crossed the Ohio had a better chance of making their way to freedom. To help slaves escape to the North, a group of free African Americans and concerned white people secretly formed the Underground Railroad. The Underground Railroad was neither a railroad nor was it underground. It was made up of several routes that escaped African Americans could take north. Along the Underground Railroad, many people hid slaves in safe places. They helped guide them to Canada, where slavery was illegal.

EXTRA! EXTRA!

The Underground Railroad may have gotten its name from an incident that took place in Kentucky. In 1830, Tice Davids, an enslaved African American, dashed for freedom, swimming the Ohio River. His owner chased him in a boat. But Davids reached the shore and disappeared. Later, the confused slaveholder declared, "It was as though he disappeared into some underground railroad."

GROWING PAINS

Between 1800 and 1850, the United States gained land west of the Mississippi River. The purchase of new territory stirred up discussion about slavery. Should slavery be allowed in the new territories and states?

The arguments went beyond slavery, however. The two parts of the United States—North and South—were following different paths. The southern states mainly produced agricultural products. Slave labor was used to do most of the work on the large plantations and

FIND OUT MORE

Many enslaved women stitched quilts. Some women wove a pattern into their quilts that was a secret code. The code passed information to escaping escapees on the Underground Railroad. Why might they have needed a secret code?

some of the smaller farms. The northern states, on the other hand, had small factories, trading companies, and businesses. Workers were paid wages and slavery was illegal. Northern and Southern people led different kinds of lives. The nation was divided.

CIVIL WAR

When Abraham Lincoln was elected president in 1860, he wanted to abolish slavery throughout the United States. The Southern states felt threatened by this. They believed that the U.S. government should not be more powerful than the state governments, and that each state should be able to make the decision on its own. In 1860, South Carolina was the first of the Southern states to secede, or break away from, the Union. Other states followed. Together they formed another country called the Confederate States of America. Jefferson Davis became the president of the Confederacy.

The tension between North and South led to the Civil War (1861–1865). In Kentucky, the saying "brother fought brother" was true. Men volunteered to fight for both sides. Many free African Americans joined the Union army.

Kentucky was a border state. The states of the Union were to Kentucky's north and the states of the Confederacy were to Kentucky's south. Many Kentuckians sided with the Confederacy, but others wanted to remain with the Union. In May 1861, Kentucky's government made an official statement—Kentucky would remain neutral and not take sides. However, by September, Union and Confederate armies were fighting in Kentucky. The legislature voted to stay in the Union. Some Kentucky leaders sided with the Confederacy, and formed their own government to join the Confederate states. President Abraham Lincoln said, "I may have God on my side, but I must have Kentucky."

Many battles were fought in Kentucky. An important battle took place at Perryville on October 8, 1863. Confederate armies had almost reached Louisville. Union troops attacked. More than seven thousand soldiers were killed or wounded. The Union army defeated the Confederate army in this battle.

Between 115,000 and 140,000 Kentuckians fought in the Civil War. Thirty thousand of Kentucky's soldiers died. On April 9, 1865, the Confederate Army surrendered to the Union Army. The war was over.

The battle of Perryville lasted only four hours but resulted in 1,600 deaths.

AFTER THE WAR

After the Civil War, the Thirteenth Amendment to the Constitution was ratified on December 6, 1865. It outlawed slavery throughout the United States.

The Fourteenth and Fifteenth Amendments and new state laws allowed African Americans to vote, marry, and serve on juries. However, to keep African Americans from using their rights as citizens, some white Southerners formed a secret organization called the Ku Klux Klan. Wearing disguises, members of this group terrorized African

Americans by burning their homes, churches, and businesses. They beat and killed many African Americans in Kentucky and other states. These constant attacks forced many African Americans to leave Kentucky for areas that would be safer for them and their families.

CITY LIFE IN THE LATE 1800s

In the years after the Civil War, Kentucky's cities grew. Many African Americans moved from the countryside to the cities. Immigrants from Germany and Ireland came, too. Some people who had lost homes in the war moved to the cities looking for work. Parks, theaters, and new schools were built in Kentucky's cities. Large cities had streetcars, telephones, and electric lights.

Kentucky was quickly changing. The first Kentucky Derby was held in Louisville in 1875. Football, basketball, and baseball teams formed and became popular. People especially loved baseball. In 1884, Pete Browning, a Louisville Eclipse baseball player, broke his favorite bat. An eighteen-year-old woodworker, Bud Hillerich, offered to make him a new one. Using the new bat, Browning made three hits the next day. Other players asked Hillerich to make them Louisville Slugger bats too. Today, Louisville Slugger is the oldest and biggest bat business in the world.

FAMOUS FIRSTS

- The cheeseburger originated in Louisville in 1934
- In 1879 Louisville pharmacist John Colgan created the first chewing gum, called Taffy Tolu
- Two Louisville sisters, Mildred and Patricia Hill, wrote the song "Happy Birthday to You"

COUNTRY RELIGION

In the 1880s, most people still lived in the country. Their lives were filled with difficult chores. Church was a place to get away from the hard work, to socialize, and to worship. Revival meetings drew Kentuckians together to listen to sermons. Before the Civil War, some church leaders even went so far as to preach against slavery.

New religious groups also came to Kentucky. The United Society of Believers in Christ's Second Appearing, a group also known as the Shakers, lived together in communities. In the early 1800s, Shakers started communities at Pleasant Hill and South Union. Shakers did not marry, nor have their own children. They adopted orphan children. However, Shakers didn't adopt enough children to keep their religious group growing. By the early 1900s, only a few Shakers remained.

COUNTRY JUSTICE

Travel was difficult in early Kentucky. Roads were not good and it took many days to ride on a horse between towns. This presented problems because almost every community wanted a local place to do legal business. As a result, Kentucky, a small state, ended up with 120 counties. In many counties, the judges, juries, victims, and the person accused of the crime all knew each other.

In the late 1800s eastern Kentucky was known for feuds. Some families didn't trust courts to punish criminals fairly, so they took revenge themselves. The most famous feud was between the Hatfield family in nearby West Virginia and the McCoy family in Kentucky. The feud started in 1882. By the time the feud ended in 1890, twelve people had been killed. Over the years, the reason for the feud was forgotten—some people say it started when a member of one family stole a hog from another family.

During the Black Patch War, tobacco farmers were often watched over by armed guards.

DANGEROUS BUSINESS

In the late 1800s and early 1900s large companies gained strength in the United States. In Kentucky, growing tobacco was an important business that was controlled by big companies.

In 1904, a large tobacco company decided to pay one low price to tobacco farmers in western Kentucky's Black Patch region. Black Patch was one kind of tobacco. Farmers didn't like the idea because they would lose money on their tobacco crops.

FIND OUT MORE

Unions such as the Planters Protective Association and United Mine Workers Union began in the early 1900s. Why were they formed? What do unions do today?

Angry farmers formed the Planters Protective Association. They refused to sell their tobacco to the companies until prices rose. However, some farmers decided to sell their tobacco anyway. A group of people called Night Riders tried to stop these farmers from selling their tobacco. They burned the farmers' fields, homes, and tobacco warehouses. About ten thousand Night Riders terrorized western Kentucky in the Black Patch Wars. The Black Patch Wars lasted four years.

Besides tobacco, coal mining was important to Kentuckians. The growth of coal mining occurred just after the Civil War when railroads were built into eastern Kentucky. Along with the railroads came people who started businesses and towns. Kentucky produced four times more coal in 1914 than it produced in 1900. However, mining was dangerous work. After breathing coal dust, some miners developed black lung disease, caused by deposits of coal dust that collect in the lungs. Other miners were crippled or killed in accidents. From 1910–1919, 754 miners died while digging coal when unsafe mines collapsed.

WORLD WAR I, WOMEN, AND PROHIBITION

During World War I (1914–1918) more than 84,000 Kentuckians went to war in Europe. Many U.S. soldiers trained at Camp Knox, which later became Fort Knox. At home, women replaced men in factories and in mines. Working gave many women a chance to become more independent. For these women, this was the first time they had ever worked away from home. After the war, many women demanded the right to vote. Not all Kentuckians agreed that women should be allowed to vote. However, the Kentucky legislature supported the Nineteenth Amendment. It became law in 1920, allowing women to vote in presidential elections for the first time.

Women had another cause—the abuse of alcohol. Tired of the problems caused by drinking, many women wanted to make liquor illegal. They supported Prohibition—the outlawing of making and selling liquor. The U.S. Congress approved the Eighteenth Amendment in 1917, and it was ratified by the states two years later. This law made it illegal to make, sell, or transport alcohol. However, making and selling bourbon whiskey was a major business in Kentucky. When making and selling liquor was outlawed across the nation, Kentucky's bourbon makers went out of business or sold bourbon secretly. Prohibition ended when the Twenty-first Amendment was ratified in 1933.

SEGREGATION LAWS

While women won more rights, African Americans lost rights that the Constitution guaranteed to them. After the Civil War, amendments to

State laws made it illegal for white people and African Americans to use the same public facilities such as water fountains.

the U.S. Constitution gave African Americans the same rights as all Americans. For a while, these laws were enforced.

Then, rulings from the U.S. Supreme Court began to limit the rights of African Americans. In 1876 the Court said that the Fifteenth Amendment didn't grant every male the right to vote. In 1896, the U.S. Supreme Court considered the case of *Plessy vs. Ferguson*. Was it legal for a state to make African Americans ride in separate railroad cars from whites? The Court ruled that it was legal if the train cars were "equal." This policy, called "separate but equal," allowed laws to be passed in many states that separated people by race.

By 1920, Kentucky and many other states passed laws that segregated—or separated—the races. African Americans in Kentucky had to use separate parks, hotels, restaurants, and even funeral parlors. They had to attend separate schools. In 1911, African-American jockeys were not allowed to ride in the Kentucky Derby. More white Southerners joined the Ku Klux Klan. The secret group became even more active in attacking African Americans.

THE GREAT DEPRESSION

Before the 1920s, coal, bourbon, and tobacco were the main parts of Kentucky's economy. Throughout the 1920s, however, these products became less profitable for the state. Kentucky sold less coal than before World War I. Also, it was illegal to make and sell bourbon whiskey. Because so much tobacco was being produced, tobacco prices dropped. The state fell on hard times.

On top of all that, in 1929 the Great Depression (1929–1939) began when the stock market crashed. Many businesses lost money and shut down. Banks closed. At least twelve million people across the nation were out of work. Many farmers couldn't pay their bank loans and the banks took over their farms.

In 1930 a drought withered crops. The lack of rain meant that many farmers couldn't raise enough crops to pay their debts. In 1937 a huge flood ruined much of Louisville, Paducah, and other towns on the Ohio River. However, many Kentucky families knew how to live from the land. Family members came home from other states to help out and Kentucky's population grew.

Meanwhile, coal miners talked about forming unions to demand safer working conditions and better pay. In 1932, miners in Harlan County asked mine owners to make the mines safer. Mine owners refused to improve the mines and hired armed guards to frighten and beat up miners. Reacting to the use of violence, many more miners began to discuss forming unions. Mine owners tried to prevent miners from forming unions. Fighting broke out. Many miners and guards who worked for the mine owners were killed. The Harlan County Coal Wars

Coal company owners used violence to prevent miners from joining unions.

ended in 1935 when new federal laws gave people the right to join unions.

WORLD WAR II

In 1939 World War II (1939–1945) started in Europe. In December 1941, the United States entered the war when the Japanese bombed Pearl Harbor, a U.S. military post in Hawaii. The war changed people's lives around the world. Things changed in Kentucky too. About 307,000 Kentuckians went to war. With many young men at war, factories needed new workers. Many Kentuckians, especially African-Americans, found jobs in the factories. Many women took factory jobs too.

Companies in Kentucky contributed to the war effort. The Louisville Slugger Company made rifle stocks instead of baseball bats. The Ford Motor Company in Louisville switched to making jeeps. A Paducah factory made ammunition. Army bases at Fort Knox and Camp Campbell swelled. The government moved the Declaration of Independence and the U.S. Constitution to the Fort Knox gold vault for safekeeping.

Fort Knox is an army post located about 31 miles (50 km) from Louisville. Gold worth billions of dollars is kept inside Fort Knox's heavily guarded U.S. Bullion Depository.

After World War II, African Americans demanded their equal rights as citizens. Laws didn't only segregate railroad cars and parks. In Kentucky, as in many other states, African-American and white children attended separate schools. The education of African-American students was not on the same level as that for white students. African-American schools received less money from the state legislature so that African-American students went to run-down schools and used old books.

In 1954, the U.S. Supreme Court ordered all states to desegregate their schools. This ruling meant that all students should now attend the same schools. At first many state legislatures refused to obey the Supreme Court ruling. However, Kentucky acted immediately to support the ruling. Kentucky was the first southern state to allow white and African-American students to attend the same schools. The state became a model for other states to follow.

In the 1960s, African Americans continued to fight for their rights. In some cities, such as Louisville and Frankfort, African Americans and their supporters protested at restaurants that refused to serve African Americans. They held sit-ins at lunch counters. They simply sat down and refused to leave until they were served. They also held up signs and blocked the doors of these restaurants. White customers would sometimes make fun of the protestors or throw things at them. Many times police officers dragged the protestors out.

These protests helped to change laws in the state. Kentucky passed the first civil rights law in the South in 1966. This law ended segrega-

tion in bathrooms, restaurants, swimming pools, and other public places. In 1968, Kentucky passed the first Fair Housing Act in the South. This law said that landowners should treat white and African Americans equally. However, in 1968, there were riots in Louisville after Dr. Martin Luther King Jr. was assassinated.

Strip mining scars the land and causes soil erosion and pollution of waterways.

CHANGES IN MINING

Many coal mine owners closed their mines rather than allow union workers. Other coal mine owners closed mines when the sale of coal went down. When coal mines closed, people who lived in the mountains of eastern Kentucky lost their jobs. By 1960, two out of five Appalachian Kentuckians lived in poverty. Several U.S. Government programs, such as Head Start and VISTA (Volunteers in Service to America), tried to help.

In the early 1960s, one third of Kentucky's coal came from strip mines. Strip miners used huge machines to strip away the topsoil in order to dig the coal. Strip-mining destroyed forests and flattened mountains. Because trees and plants were removed in strip-mining, water poured off the land and washed away chemicals and soil. Nearby rivers and streams became polluted.

In 1966, Kentucky passed tougher strip-mining laws. These laws forced mining companies to replant trees. The federal government passed more laws in the 1970s. Referred to as "Reclamation," the goal of these laws was to restore mined land to its original state. Today, there are fewer strip mines in Kentucky.

KENTUCKY LEGENDS

Some Kentuckians became household names in the 1950s and 1960s. Adolf F. Rupp coached the University of Kentucky basketball team to a record 129 home court winning streak. Muhammad Ali became boxing's heavyweight champion of the world in 1964. That year Colonel Harland D. Sanders sold his Kentucky Fried Chicken company (now KFC) for two million dollars. The face of Colonel Sanders is recognized around the world.

Kentucky changed with the times. In 1983, Kentucky elected Martha Layne Collins, one of the first female governors in the United States. In the early 1980s, only about half of Kentuckians had graduated from high school. Collins asked the state legislature for more money for schools.

In 1989, the Kentucky State Supreme Court forced more change. A portion of local taxes usually pays for schools. That means rich areas can spend more money on schools than poor areas can. The court ruled that Kentucky's government needed to make sure all students received an equal education no matter where they lived. The state passed the Kentucky Education Reform Act. Now the legislature provides more money for schools. Pay for teachers has gone up and nearly every classroom has computers.

In the 1990s and more recently, Kentucky has also taken more interest in cleaning up the environment. In 1991 the legislature passed the Solid Waste Management Act. This law limited the amount of garbage that companies in other states could dump in Kentucky. Until 2000 mountain hollows in forty eastern counties had many illegal dumps. Usually the dumps contained tons of garbage, rusted car parts, and pipes that spilled raw sewage into creeks. An organization of volunteers called PRIDE (Personal

EXTRA! EXTRA!

Harland Sanders was born in Henryville, Indiana in 1890. He learned to cook at age six when his father died and his mother went to work. Later, he cooked for travelers at his service station in Corbin. In 1952, Sanders began traveling around the country cooking chicken for restaurant owners. If they wanted to use his recipe, they agreed to pay him a nickel for every chicken dinner they sold.

Responsibility in a Desirable Environment) has been cleaning up these dumps. Of the 1,996 dumps in the eastern counties, about 377 had been cleaned up by the end of 2000. State legislators also considered a law that would force people to clean up the environment.

In this century, people in Kentucky will continue to protect the environment. They will also be considering the best ways to educate their children. One of the problems that Kentuckians will face is how to pay for all the things that need to be done. A portion of the money raised from the Kentucky Lottery goes to education. Some states have also turned to legal gambling in order to raise money for the state. In 2007, Kentuckians elected Steven Beshear to be governor. He has promised to bring gambling casinos to the state.

New technology and ideas are changing Kentucky. Health-conscious Americans smoke less and laws against smoking in public places have been passed throughout the nation. Some tobacco farmers have given up growing tobacco. Now they raise soybeans or other crops. As is happening in all parts of the world, the Internet connects Kentucky's schools, businesses, and families to the rest of the modern, global community.

CHAPTER FOUR

GOVERNING KENTUCKY

Kentucky is called a commonwealth. That is another word for state. It means "for the common good." Kentucky's constitution, adopted in 1891, is modeled after the U.S. Constitution. The constitution divides the government into three branches—the executive, the legislative, and the judicial.

The state capitol is considered one of the most beautiful in the nation.

THE EXECUTIVE BRANCH

The governor is the leader of the executive branch. He and his staff make sure state laws are enforced and carried out. They suggest new laws and plans. Kentucky's governor is elected for a four-year term. The governor can serve a second term, if elected again. Other state officers are elected, too. A cabinet, a group of experts, helps the governor. Cabinet officials are not elected. The governor chooses, or appoints, them.

EXTRA! EXTRA!

A state constitution provides the framework or skeleton for the government. It gives the rules that the government must follow. Kentucky is governed by its fourth constitution. This constitution was adopted in 1891.

The state senate meets in this chamber.

THE LEGISLATIVE BRANCH

Legislators make the laws for the state. They make laws that they think will help Kentuckians. For example, they make laws about race horses, tobacco, highways, school safety, and even what the state dog will be. They decide how much money the state needs and how much tax to charge people.

The legislature is called the General Assembly. It has two houses. Kentucky's 100 representatives are elected for two-year terms. The 38 senators are elected to serve for four-year terms.

Kentucky legislators meet once a year for thirty or sixty days. Between sessions, lawmakers meet in special committees. Each committee focuses on a subject such as education or building contracts. Committees plan laws to suggest when the legislature meets.

THE JUDICIAL BRANCH

Members of the judicial branch interpret the laws. Often they decide exactly what a law means. Kentucky Supreme Court Justices compare laws to the state constitution. If they think the law goes against what the constitution allows, they say the law is unconstitutional, or illegal. Judges supervise the courts. They make sure trials are fair.

The judicial branch is called the Kentucky Court of Justice. It is made up of four courts—district, circuit, appeals, and supreme. Kentucky courts handle civil and criminal cases. A criminal case concerns a crime such as stealing, murder, or jaywalking. Criminal cases for serious crimes, such as murder, are called felonies. Cases for smaller crimes, such as shoplifting, are called misdemeanors. Civil cases are different. They concern disagreements between two parties about money, property, or business agreements.

In Kentucky, district courts hear cases about traffic tickets, misdemeanors, and civil cases involving less than $4,000. Circuit courts hear murder and felony cases, and civil cases concerning more than $4,000. The Court of Appeals considers cases that have already been tried in district or circuit court. The person that disagrees with the decision can ask the Court of Appeals, a higher court, to review the case. The Supreme Court, the highest court in the state, may review decisions from the Court of Appeals. It may also review laws to decide if they are constitutional. Kentucky also has family courts. They only hear cases involving children and their families.

KENTUCKY STATE GOVERNMENT

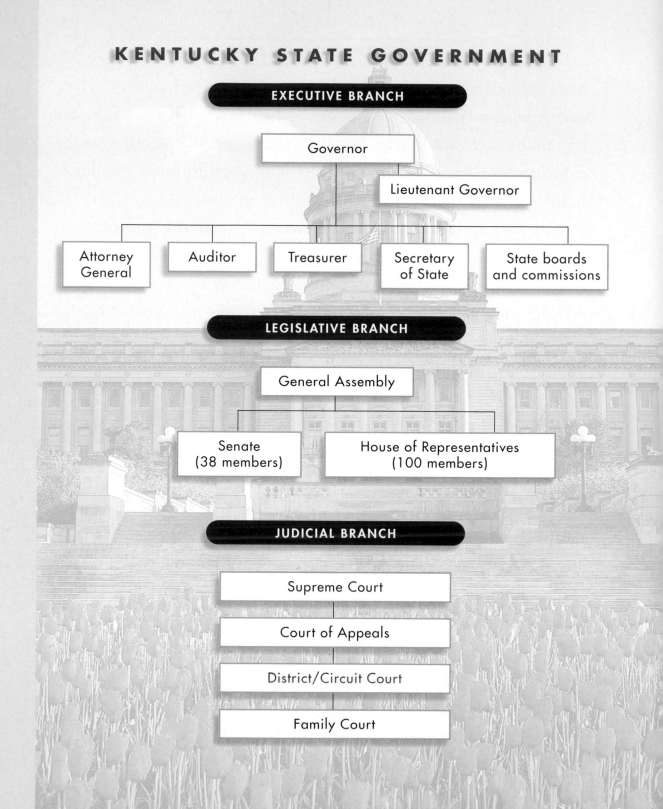

EXECUTIVE BRANCH

Governor

Lieutenant Governor

Attorney General

Auditor

Treasurer

Secretary of State

State boards and commissions

LEGISLATIVE BRANCH

General Assembly

Senate (38 members)

House of Representatives (100 members)

JUDICIAL BRANCH

Supreme Court

Court of Appeals

District/Circuit Court

Family Court

KENTUCKY GOVERNORS

Name	Term	Name	Term
Isaac Shelby	1792–1796	John Young Brown	1891–1895
James Garrard	1796–1804	William O'Connell Bradley	1895–1899
Christopher Greenup	1804–1808	William Sylvester Taylor	1899–1900
Charles Scott	1808–1812	William Goebel	1900
Isaac Shelby	1812–1816	John Crepps Wickliffe Beckham	1900–1907
George Madison	1816	Augustus Everett Willson	1907–1911
Gabriel Slaughter	1816–1820	James Bennett McCreary	1911–1915
John Adair	1820–1824	Augustus O. Stanley	1915–1919
Joseph Desha	1824–1828	James Dixon Black	1919
Thomas Metcalfe	1828–1832	Edwin Porch Morrow	1919–1923
John Breahitt	1832–1834	William Jason Fields	1923–1927
James Turner Morehead	1834–1836	Flem D. Sampson	1927–1931
James Clark	1836–1839	Ruby Laffoon	1931–1935
Charles Anderson Wickliffe	1839–1840	Albert Benjamin Chandler	1635–1939
Robert Perkins Letcher	1840–1844	Keen Johnson	1939–1943
William Owsley	1844–1848	Simeon Willis	1943–1947
John Jordan Crittenden	1848–1850	Earle Chester Clements	1947–1950
John Larue Helm	1850–1851	Lawrence Winchester Wetherby	1950–1955
Lazarus Whitehead Powell	1851–1855	Albert Benjamin Chandler	1955–1959
Charles Slaughter Morehead	1855–1859	Bert T. Combs	1959–1963
Beriah Magoffin	1859–1862	Edward Thompson Breathitt Jr.	1963–1967
George W. Johnson	1861–1862*	Louie Broady Nunn	1967–1971
James Fisher Robinson	1862–1863	Wendell Hampton Ford	1971–1974
Richard Hawes	1862–1865*	Julian Morton Carroll	1974–1979
Thomas Elliott Bramlette	1863–1867	John Brown Jr.	1979–1983
John White Stevenson	1867–1871	Martha Layne Collins	1983–1987
Preston Hopkins Leslie	1871–1875	Wallace Glenn Wilkinson	1987–1991
James Bennett McCreary	1875–1879	Brereton C. Jones	1991–1995
Luke Pryor Blackburn	1879–1883	Paul E. Patton	1995–2003
James Proctor Knott	1883–1887	Ernie Fletcher	2003–2008
Simon Bolivar Buckner	1887–1891	Steven L. Beshear	2008–

*Confederate state governors

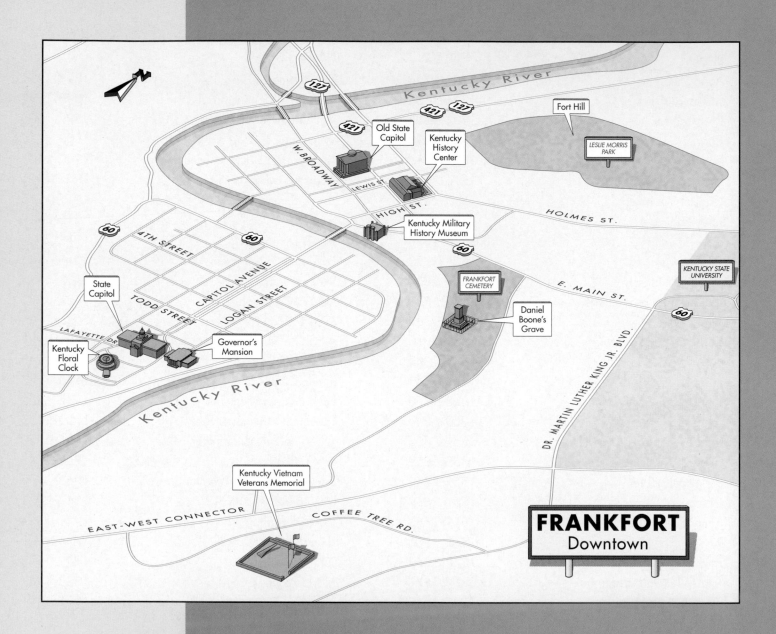

TAKE A TOUR OF FRANKFORT, THE CAPITAL CITY

In 1792, there wasn't much money to build a state capital in Kentucky. Towns bid for the honor. Frankfort offered a big house, building lots, 1,500 pounds (680.39 kg) of nails and other materials, plus $3,000. Frankfort's bid and central location won. Today, Frankfort isn't Kentucky's biggest city. It had only 26,418 people in 1998. It is important, however, because it is the capital.

Today's capitol building was built in 1910. Inside, along with the meeting rooms, are statues of important Kentuckians and also the First Lady Doll Collection. The collection's dolls look like each of Kentucky's governor's wives, the first ladies. Walk outside and you'll see a clock made of 10,000 flowers and plants. It is 34 feet (10.36 m) across. Its 20-foot long (6.1-meter) hands weigh 500 pounds (226.8 kgm) each.

What else can you do in Frankfort? Visit Frankfort Cemetery to see Daniel Boone's gravestone. Or, go to the Kentucky History Museum. A

Here is an inside view of the capitol building.

49

The giant floral clock is surrounded by a reflecting pool.

The Kentucky Vietnam Veterans Memorial has a sundial and a granite panel on which the names of Kentuckians killed in the Vietnam War are etched.

FIND OUT MORE

Kentucky, like most states, wanted its capital near the center of the state. Can you guess why?

display with trees and animal noises is just inside the door. You'll feel like you've walked through the Cumberland Gap!

You can also tour the governor's home, Kentucky State University, the Kentucky History Center, or poke around Civil War earth barricades on Fort Hill. Above the city is another clock. It is a sundial. The names of Kentuckians killed in Vietnam are carved in its base. The sundial's shadow touches each name on the anniversary of the soldier's death.

CHAPTER FIVE

THE PEOPLE AND PLACES OF KENTUCKY

Would you like a big plate of fried chicken, grits (first made from Native Americans' corn), or okra (from Africa originally)? How about a steaming bowl of burgoo, a thick stew that originated from Native American or French trapper recipes? In Kentucky, you could sample corn cakes fried as they are in Scotland, or sweet corn pudding. If you're lucky, you'll try beaten biscuits, which are made by beating dough over and over again. Kentucky tradition holds you can beat them with a rolling pin, a tire iron, or, as one family claims, "Granny used to beat 'em with a musket." Read the menu of Kentucky foods and you'll see who has lived in Kentucky. Each group —Native American, African-American, Scotch Irish—brought their cooking traditions.

Country music is very popular in Kentucky.

One of the great foods of Kentucky is beaten biscuits.

African Americans make up a small but growing part of Kentucky's population.

Over the years, Kentucky's population has changed. Once, almost one-fourth of Kentucky's people were African American. In 2000, only about seven people out of every hundred were African Americans. Only one in one thousand Kentuckians is Native American. Seven in a thousand have an Asian background. Eight per thousand trace their families to Latin America. In Kentucky, such as in many rural states, about ninety out of every hundred people are Caucasian. Kentucky has fewer immigrants than many other states. About seventy-seven out of a hundred Kentuckians were born in the state.

WORKING IN KENTUCKY

Would you like to be an auctioneer? In Kentucky, you could go to tobacco auctioneer's school where you'll learn how to auction off, or sell, tobacco to interested buyers. Kentucky grows more tobacco than any other state except North Carolina. In 2006, Kentucky's exported crop was worth $295 million. Other important crops are soybeans, corn, and cattle. About one-third of Kentucky's land, 13,900,000 acres (56,251 sq km), is farmland. Kentucky's farms are often small. However, with 91,000 farms, the state's farmers sold $3,632,928 worth of crops in 1999.

Kentuckians have many kinds of jobs besides auctioneering and farming. About eighteen out of every hundred people work in factories making cars, farm machinery, and clothes. Kentucky has more factory workers for its size than most other states. Ford, General Motors, and Toyota plants make Kentucky a major auto-

mobile producer. Some Kentuckians work in book and magazine publishing, and other print materials. Louisville's American Printing House for the Blind, which started in 1858, is the oldest publisher for the blind in the United States.

Many people work in Kentucky's steel mills.

(opposite)
Tobacco hangs and dries in a barn.

Although Kentucky has fewer coal mines today, many people still earn their living working in the mines.

Fewer and fewer Kentuckians work in coal mines. Because of the decline in coal sales between 1984 and 1999, almost three out of four mines closed. In 1974, there were almost 50,000 miners in Kentucky. By 2000, only about 15,500 people worked in mines. Although Kentucky still produces 130.6 tons of coal per year, machines do much of the work. Many miners have had to find other kinds of work. Some eastern Kentuckians have turned to making traditional crafts such as quilts, weavings, pottery, and baskets for sale to tourists and people across the country.

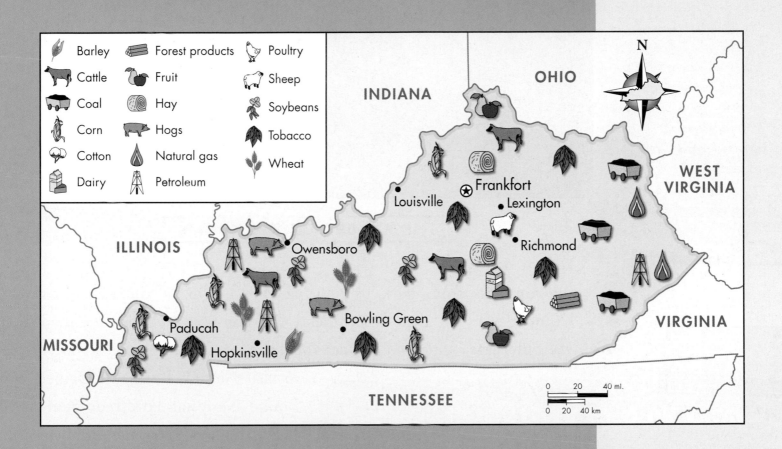

Barley
Cattle
Coal
Corn
Cotton
Dairy
Forest products
Fruit
Hay
Hogs
Natural gas
Petroleum
Poultry
Sheep
Soybeans
Tobacco
Wheat

INDIANA

OHIO

N

WEST VIRGINIA

ILLINOIS

Louisville

Frankfort

Lexington

Richmond

VIRGINIA

Owensboro

MISSOURI

Paducah

Hopkinsville

Bowling Green

TENNESSEE

0   20   40 ml.

0   20   40 km

What else do Kentuckians do? Some work with horses. Kentucky produced 9,800 thoroughbred foals in 2002—more than any other state. About 52,000 Kentuckians worked on horse farms or in the racing business. Today, many workers on horse farms are immigrants from Ireland or Mexico.

THE PLACES OF KENTUCKY

Eastern Mountains

As you pass from dark to light at the mouth of the tunnel at Cumberland Gap, there is Kentucky. Can you imagine when the road was only large enough for a mule? You'll need your hiking boots in order to visit Natural Bridge in Daniel Boone National Forest or Kentucky's highest waterfall, Cumberland Falls. If it's nighttime and the moon is full, look for the moonbow arching across the falls.

Craft centers at Fall Mountain, David, or Vest sell bright quilts

WHO'S WHO IN KENTUCKY?

Martha Bell. When Martha Bell was ten years old, she checked in every day on a sick woman her family knew in McCracken County. Today, Martha Bell runs Martha's Vineyard in Paducah. This organization provides free meals to homeless people and people who are too sick to leave their homes. In one day, the organization might serve 460 meals in their dining room, plus deliver more on fifteen routes in the county. Martha says, "God just gave me the vision of doing it and I started."

and intricate carvings. The people of Kentucky's mountains, many of whose families have lived here for generations, bring tradition to life. Time seems frozen until you come across the monster trucks, cranes, and machinery of a coal mine. You can also hear the music of Dulcimers throughout Kentucky. Dulcimers are stringed folk instruments dating back many years in history.

This natural arch is found in Daniel Boone National Forest.

National park, forest, or recreation area

Highway

Capital city

City

Tourist site

INDIANA

OHIO

Covington

N

71 75

Frankfort Georgetown 64 Ashland WEST VIRGINIA

ILLINOIS

Louisville

Lexington COMBS MTN. PKWY.

Fort Knox Military Reservation 65 BLUE GRASS PKWY.

Owensboro Bardstown Richmond DANIEL BOONE NATIONAL FOREST JEFFERSON NATIONAL FOREST

MAMMOTH CAVE NATIONAL PARK Hodgenville

NATCHER PKWY.

LAND BETWEEN THE LAKES NATIONAL RECREATION AREA

Abraham Lincoln Birthplace National Historic Site Renfro Valley 75

Paducah Horse Cave

MISSOURI Hopkinsville Corbin

65 Bowling Green

24 Fort Campbell Military Res. Harlan VIRGINIA

PURCHASE PKWY.

TENNESSEE

CUMBERLAND GAP NATIONAL HISTORICAL PARK

0   20   40 mi.
0   20   40 km

Bluegrass Region

The Bluegrass Region is home to most of Kentucky's people and a lot of horses. Here you will find the cities of Lexington, Louisville, and Frankfort.

At Lexington, you can visit the Kentucky Horse Park to see all breeds of horses, a horse museum, or even attend BreyerFest, a model horse festival. Every year thousands of model horse collectors come to BreyerFest to buy, sell, and trade models. The American Saddlebred Museum is nearby. An interactive screen allows you to see what you would look like while sitting on an American Saddlebred

The Horse Farm Museum attracts many visitors.

horse. While you're in Lexington, try to get tickets to a Wildcats basketball game at the University of Kentucky. The Wildcats have been national basketball champs seven times. They usually play at Rupp Arena.

In Georgetown, take a tour of Toyota's automobile factory. Put on safety glasses and board the tram. This ride takes you through the factory where cars are welded and assembled.

Fans find thrills at a
Wildcats game.

Do you like history? Fort Boonesborough looks much as it did when Daniel Boone lived there. If you visit Shaker Village at Pleasantville, you can see how Shakers lived in the 1800s. You'll hear Shaker music in the meeting house. You can take classes in blacksmithing or see where Civil War soldiers once camped.

Just south of Lexington is a town called Berea. Berea is called "The Folk Arts and Crafts Capital of Kentucky." You can browse through shops filled with unique crafts like baskets, cornshuck dolls, quilts, and pottery.

Now let's go on to Louisville. Each May, crowds pack Louisville's Churchill Downs for the Kentucky Derby. The Derby Festival, held in the weeks before the race, features hot air balloon races, fireworks, and The Great Steamboat Race. The steamboat race began in 1963 and has become one of the festival's most popular events. Crowds gather to watch as Louisville's historic steamer, the Belle of Louisville, races against New Orleans' Delta Queen. The race celebrates the days when river commerce and travel were impor-

At Shaker Village, visitors can see how the earliest Shakers did everything from weaving to farming.

The lights of Louisville sparkle above the Ohio River.

tant to Kentucky. The Louisville Slugger Museum is nearby. Watch for the 120-foot steel baseball bat at the entrance. Don't try picking it up—the bat weighs 6,800 pounds (3,084 kgm). One display makes you feel as if a ninety mile (144.8 km) per hour pitch is coming at you. Afterward, you can tour the baseball bat factory.

The Louisville Zoo has one of the largest spider collections in the United States. Look for the baby giraffe born in 2000. The Louisville Science Center has hands-on activities, a Space Science Gallery, and a KidZone, a hands-on exhibit for young children.

You can almost hear the galloping hooves in this photo of the Kentucky Derby.

If you love roller coasters, go to Six Flags Kentucky Kingdom near the Kentucky Fair and Exhibition Center. This amusement park has 110 rides and attractions. Chang is the longest, tallest, fastest, stand-up roller coaster in the world. It is 154 feet (46.9 m) long and 4,155 feet (1,266.4 m) high. It whips riders around at a top speed of 63 miles (101 km) per hour.

Tour the American Printing House for the Blind to see how books are made in Braille. One of the guides will show you how to write your name in Braille.

The Louisville Slugger Factory produces the best-known baseball bats.

Covington and Newport are across the Ohio River from Cincinnati. At these cities, you can enjoy the Tall Stacks Festival. Riverboats from up and down the Ohio and Mississippi steam to the festival. There are riverboat races and historic exhibits. Storytellers in costumes from riverboat days tell tall tales. Besides steamboats, Covington also has great German food. Main-Strasse Village in Covington is a neighborhood that looks just like one that may have existed in Germany two hundred years ago. As you visit the shops, note the Goose Girl Fountain. It has a life-size statue of a German girl carrying two geese to market.

Pennyroyal

In the Pennyroyal in southwestern Kentucky, you can go underground in Mammoth Cave National Park. There are more than 350 miles (563 km) of underground passages here. Grab your jacket because it's cold down there. The caves stay about 60°F (15.6° C) year-round. Guides take you through the underground wonders of pale pink and peach caverns. Water drips overhead. In the farthest reaches of the cave live colorless spiders and blind fish. The fish are blind because of the cave's immense darkness, which makes eyes unnecessary.

Kentucky pioneers found lots of ways to use corn, which was a staple in their gardens. Today, corn pudding is still a classic Kentucky side dish. This rich casserole is one of everybody's favorites. Remember to ask an adult for help.

KENTUCKY CORN PUDDING

1 cup corn kernels
1/4 cup flour
4 tsp. sugar
1/4 tsp. salt
2 tbsp. melted butter
2 cups milk
2 eggs

1. Mix the corn, flour, salt, sugar and melted butter in a large bowl.
2.. In another bowl, beat the eggs and add the milk.
3. Pour the milk mixture into the corn mixture and stir.
4. Bake in a shallow baking dish at 450°F for 40 minutes.
5. Stir the pudding gently after 10 minutes and again after 20 minutes. Continue cooking.
6. Serve it hot!

About two million people visit Mammoth Cave each year.

You can visit Abraham Lincoln's birthplace or the Lincoln Museum near Hodgenville. In October, go to Penn's Country Store in Gravel Switch, where you can join the crowd gathered for the Great Outhouse Blowout. An outhouse is a small building, separate from a main building, that was used as a toilet in the old days. How do outhouses race? They are on wheels. Teams of five people push them 300 feet (91.4 m) to the finish line. The race began in 1993 to celebrate the addition of a working outhouse to Penn's Country Store.

Western Kentucky

Can you imagine a steamboat chugging down the river? Towns like Paducah and Henderson are still ports, although the ships are bigger. Near Henderson is the James Audubon State Park, where the famous artist lived and worked. Are you a Scout? Try the ropes course at the National Scouting Museum in Murray.

At Paducah, you can visit the American Quilt Museum or go to beautiful, green Land Between the Lakes Park. Half of the park is located in Kentucky and the other half in Tennessee. Lake Barkley and Kentucky Lake surround Land Between the Lakes. Pitch your tent. Look up at the stars. Mississippian people, Chickasaw, riverboat captains, and African-American slaves have all done the same.

From Daniel Boone to Muhammad Ali, it's Kentucky. Drop a postcard home: *Wish you were here. Glad I came!*

KENTUCKY ALMANAC

Statehood date and number: June 1, 1792; 15th

State seal: 1792

State flag: approved 1928

Geographic center: Marion County, 3 miles N-NW of Lebanon

Total area/rank: 40,409 square miles (104,659 square kilometers)/37th

Borders: Tennessee, Virginia, West Virginia, Indiana, Illinois, Missouri

Highest/lowest elevation: Black Mountain, 4,145 feet (1,264 m)/Fulton County, 257 ft (78 m)

Hottest/coldest temperature: 114°F (46°C) at Greensburg on July 28, 1930/-37°F (-38°C) on January 19, 1994

Land area/rank: 39,728 sq mi (102,896 sq km)/36th

Population/rank: 4,041,769 (2000 Census)/22nd

Population of major cities:

   Louisville: 256,231

   Lexington-Fayette: 260,512

   Owensboro: 54,067

   Bowling Green: 49,296

   Covington: 43,370

Origin of state name: Of Native American origin, possibly from an Iroquoian word "*Ken-tah-ten*" meaning "land of tomorrow"

State capital: Frankfort

Previous capitals: None

Counties: 120

State government: 38 senators, 100 representatives

Major rivers, lakes: Tennessee, Ohio, Kentucky, Cumberland, Green, Lake Barkley, Kentucky Lake, Lake Cumberland

Farm products:
   Tobacco, corn, soybeans, wheat, oats, barley, rye

Livestock: Beef cattle, horses, hogs, broiler chickens

Manufactured products: Farm machinery, whiskey, cigarettes, plumbing fixtures, electrical goods, food-processing machines, household appliances, paper and food products, heating equipment

Mining products: Coal, lime, sand and gravel, clays, crushed stone, Portland cement

Bird: Cardinal

Butterfly: Viceroy

Dog: Beagle

Fish: Kentucky bass

Flower: Goldenrod

Fossil: Brachiopod

Horse: Thoroughbred

Gemstone: Fresh-water pearl

Mineral: Coal

Motto: "United we stand. Divided we fall."

Nickname: Bluegrass State

Soil: Crider soil series

Song: "My Old Kentucky Home," by Stephen Foster

Tree: Tulip poplar

TIME**LINE**

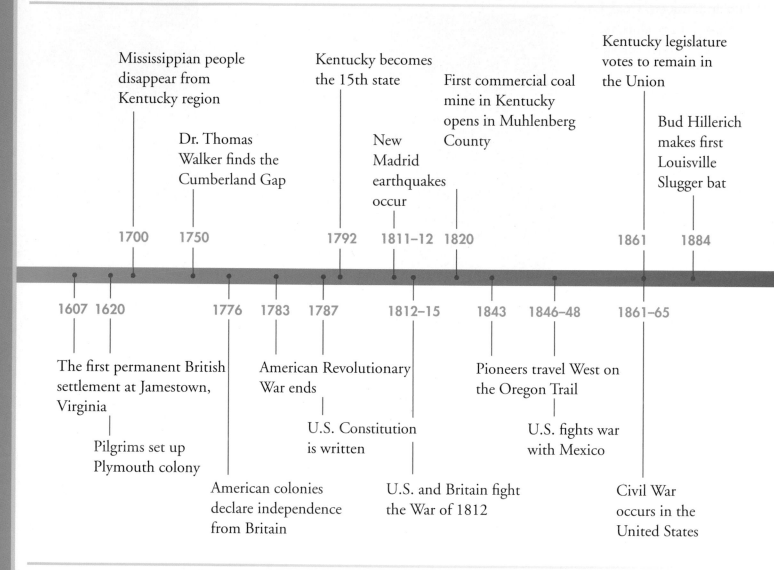

Mississippian people disappear from Kentucky region

Kentucky becomes the 15th state

First commercial coal mine in Kentucky opens in Muhlenberg County

Kentucky legislature votes to remain in the Union

Dr. Thomas Walker finds the Cumberland Gap

New Madrid earthquakes occur

Bud Hillerich makes first Louisville Slugger bat

1700   1750   1792   1811–12 1820   1861   1884

1607 1620   1776   1783   1787   1812–15   1843   1846–48   1861–65

The first permanent British settlement at Jamestown, Virginia

American Revolutionary War ends

Pioneers travel West on the Oregon Trail

Pilgrims set up Plymouth colony

U.S. Constitution is written

U.S. fights war with Mexico

American colonies declare independence from Britain

U.S. and Britain fight the War of 1812

Civil War occurs in the United States

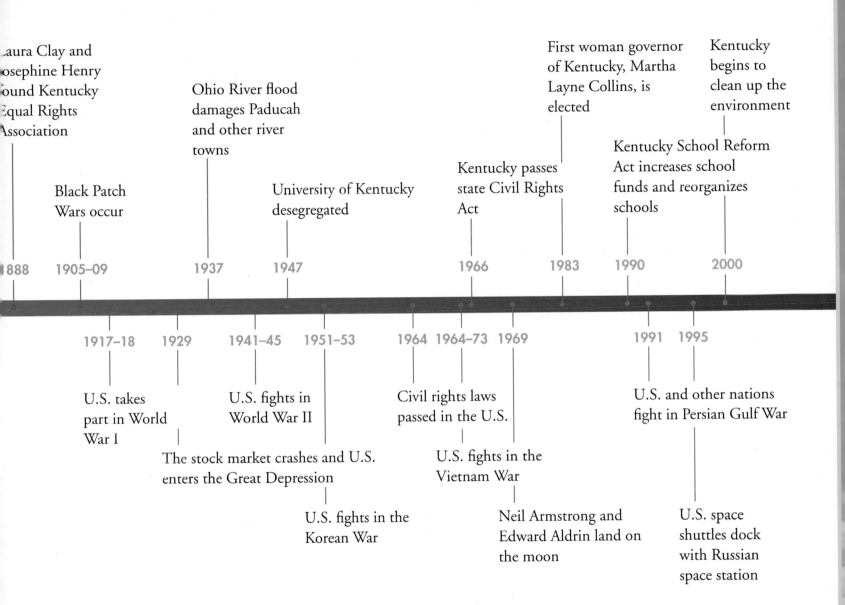

Laura Clay and
Josephine Henry
found Kentucky
Equal Rights
Association

Black Patch
Wars occur

Ohio River flood
damages Paducah
and other river
towns

University of Kentucky
desegregated

Kentucky passes
state Civil Rights
Act

First woman governor
of Kentucky, Martha
Layne Collins, is
elected

Kentucky School Reform
Act increases school
funds and reorganizes
schools

Kentucky
begins to
clean up the
environment

1888   1905–09   1937   1947   1966   1983   1990   2000

1917–18   1929   1941–45   1951–53   1964 1964–73 1969   1991 1995

U.S. takes
part in World
War I

U.S. fights in
World War II

Civil rights laws
passed in the U.S.

U.S. and other nations
fight in Persian Gulf War

The stock market crashes and U.S.
enters the Great Depression

U.S. fights in the
Vietnam War

U.S. fights in the
Korean War

Neil Armstrong and
Edward Aldrin land on
the moon

U.S. space
shuttles dock
with Russian
space station

GALLERY OF FAMOUS KENTUCKIANS

Muhammad Ali
(1942–)
Three time heavyweight champion boxer. Born in Louisville.

Daniel Boone
(1734–1820)
Kentucky frontiersman and explorer. Born in Pennsylvania.

William Wells Brown
(1814–1884)
Abolitionist and writer. The first African-American to publish a novel. Born near Lexington.

Henry Clay
(1777–1852)
U.S. Senator from Kentucky. Born in Virginia.

Abraham Lincoln
(1809–1865)
Sixteenth United States president. Born in Hardin County.

Loretta Lynn
(1935–)
Famous country singer. The movie *Coal Miner's Daughter* tells her life story. Born in Butcher Hollow.

Mary T. Meagher
(1964–)
Olympic swimmer and world record breaker. Born in Louisville.

Garrett Morgan
(1877–1963)
Entrepreneur and inventor. Born in Paris.

Wes Unseld
(1946–)
NBA basketball player and manager. Born in Louisville.

Brian Littrell
(1975–)
Member of the Backstreet Boys singing group. Born in Lexington.

GLOSSARY

abolitionist: a person opposed to slavery

appeal: to ask a higher court to review a lower court decision

census: official government count of population

deed: legal document stating land ownership

descendent: child, grandchild, or following generations of a person, family, or nationality

feud: long-lasting argument, often bloody, between members of different families

flatboat: roughly built flat-bottomed boat

integration: act of including people of different races in the same places and activities

karst: an underground landscape of caves, underground drainage, and sinkholes

Ku Klux Klan: secret society formed to oppose African-Americans and other groups

legislature: group of people elected to make laws

Melungeon: Group of dark-skinned, blue-eyed people from the Kentucky mountains

militia: a group of a state's citizens organized for protection

patent: a government paper giving a person legal rights to an invention or idea

Prohibition: a law making selling or using liquor illegal; the time in U.S. history when liquor was illegal

prosper: to succeed and make money

secede: to quit a group

segregation: the act of keeping people of different races separate

treaty: an agreement between two governments that they both must obey

Underground Railroad: secret routes that escaped slaves followed to freedom

Union: an organization of workers formed to bargain with employers for better wages and/or working conditions

FOR MORE INFORMATION

Web sites

4 Your Info, A Courier Journal Site
www.courier-journal.com/nie/nieforyourinfo.html
All about Kentucky for kids including stories and book reviews by children in Kentucky.

Kentucky Legislature Home Page
www.lrc.ky.gov
Information about Kentucky's legislature, including a special kids' section that includes photos and stories.

Kentucky Tales
www.kytales.com
Cartoons of Kentucky's heritage, just for kids.

Books

Bial, Raymond. *Shaker Home.* New York, NY: Houghton Mifflin, 1994.

Lawlor, Laurie. *Daniel Boone.* Niles, IL: Albert Whitman and Company, 1988.

Wells, Rosemary. *Mary on Horseback, Three Mountain Stories.* New York, NY: Viking Press, 1999.

Addresses

Kentucky Tourism Council
1100 127 South, Building C
Frankfort, KY 40601

Kentucky Chamber of Commerce
P.O. Box 817
Frankfort, KY 40602

Kentucky Historical Society
100 West Broadway
Frankfort, KY 40601

INDEX

MEET THE AUTHOR

Suzanne M. Williams' grandmother used to tell her stories about growing up near Paducah, Kentucky. Suzanne grew up in California and lives in Nevada. She has three children, a couple of dogs, and a cranky cat. She used to teach elementary school, but now writes children's books.

To write this book, Suzanne talked to people in Kentucky and had books from across the country sent to her local library. She also found that the Internet is full of information on Kentucky.